Old School

Leadership Wisdoms

By Gary Hassenstab

ISBN:1537116061
ISBN-13:9781537116068

ACKNOWLEDGEMENTS

Much appreciation to three leaders who coached and mentored me during my first formal leadership roles. The consistency with which you all "walked the talk" and created empowered and engaged teams that were accountable for the success of the organization was the hallmark of your leadership.
So, to Bob Nelson, Chuck Walton, and Norm Oshiro – thanks guys.

Thanks also to Brent Meers and Cindy Canevaro, my colleagues and coaches at EDS Executive Development, who helped me translate the words of the leadership values into observable actions.

Thanks to Carly Hassenstab for editing my rough drafts and showing me how to begin a simple sentence.

OLD SCHOOL LEADERSHIP WISDOMS:

DUSTED OFF, RE-EXAMINED, AND REFRESHED FOR THE 21ST CENTURY.

CONTENTS

INTRODUCTION

I got my first leadership role at EDS in 1985 as a supervisor over a team of System Engineers. An example of the old adage with an IT twist - those who can code do, those that can't become supervisors and managers. It was at that point that I was introduced to the, "EDS Grass Roots Wisdoms of Leadership". These wisdoms represented the EDS approach to being a leader since the early days of the company. Everyone who became a formal organizational leader in EDS was given and expected to lead their teams according to these simple and clear directives.

These are the wisdoms that I am now labeling as a set of "old school leadership practices". These wisdoms and practices, 30 years later, still have a great deal of relevance to the leadership needs of the 21st century organization, and the post-boomer generations that comprise a large majority of the workforce.

The story of Ross Perot and EDS is a tale of a smart visionary leader who recognized a need and an opportunity in the technology services space in the 1960's. He defined a new source of IT services, and then created the delivery and services organizations that focused on providing value via efficiencies in IT services that customers could not generate themselves.

Essentially what Mr. Perot and his leadership team built became the foundation for today's technology service offerings such as cloud computing and on and offshore services outsourcing. Mr. Perot was certainly colorful, but also, based on his Naval Academy training, understood the power of effective, consistent, disciplined, and positive leadership in an organization. The success and market leadership of EDS for three decades was because of a disciplined, results-focused organization with leaders aligned to the values and leadership practices built in the early days. A new leader was given these wisdoms on a small card, usually during the first leadership class required of all leaders.

I have kept these wisdoms close by during my career in various leadership roles, including as a leadership analyst and coach for the EDS Executive Development Program. I know that these wisdoms still have relevance almost 50 years after they were first practiced. In the following chapters I will explain each wisdom and make a case (hopefully obvious case) that these simple philosophies can still make for more effective leaders through more disciplined and clear leadership behaviors and values that perpetuate highly effective, empowered, and aligned teams and organizations. So, these are not wisdoms to make you a star. These are wisdoms to enable you to make stars of those people in your organization for whom you have been given stewardship for their engagement and, ultimately, value to the organization. These wisdoms are not a stunning new revelation on how to effectively lead. But, these basic concise leadership behaviors have been restated over several decades. Hence, the term "old school" to describe them.

The wisdoms are as follows:

1. Be honest, upfront, and candid.
2. Leaders are in charge.
3. Leaders are not obligated to perpetuate foolishness.
4. Leaders must choose which problem(s) to live with. There are very few perfect solutions.
5. Run the company (i.e. your team or organization) so the best people love it.
6. Sit in the grandstand. Get all the perspectives on the situation.
7. Run your business/project like it's your company. Is it important enough that you would pay for it?
8. No second chance to make a first impression, but you are always making an impression.
9. Bad news, unlike wine and cheese, does not get better with age. See #'s 2 and 3 above.
10. If your people are not doing what you want, it's your fault. See #2 above.

These are "truisms" that reflect Ross Perot's philosophy, leadership and the style that he desired in his leaders. These wisdoms were the foundation for EDS leadership training in the 1970's and 1980's.

I end each chapter with a reflection to help you internalize the wisdom and actually put the wisdom into practice in your approach to leading your teams. I encourage you to find some time during the day or week to think back on how you acted, interacted, made decisions, worked with your teams, etc. Consider yourself to be "practicing" leadership. The purpose of practice is to learn from your performance in the role and identify what you did well and when you missed the mark on how you wanted to perform as a leader. Make the time to observe and learn from yourself. Even 10-15 minutes thinking back on the day will get you in the habit of being an active learner of your own behaviors. For the really brave, find a partner, coach, or mentor and review these reflections with that person. But, the key is to at least start by asking yourself questions and giving yourself honest, upfront, and candid answers. So, let's start in Chapter 1 with what being honest, upfront, and candid really means.

1

WISDOM #1

BE HONEST, UPFRONT, AND CANDID

Let's begin with the first wisdom and where effective leaders must start: a personal decision to operate with honesty, openness, and deal candidly with everyone in the organization. This is not an earth-shattering or a revolutionary idea by any means. But the concept of being honest seems to derail more leaders and degrade the productivity, passion, and engagement of their teams. Following the wisdom of honesty naturally brings along the two behaviors of being upfront and candid. The first wisdom is therefore to be honest, upfront, and candid.

This wisdom is ultimately about RESPECT, meaning giving respect to your team and peers at all times by dealing with them honestly. As a leader, do you respect others, by being honest, open and candid with them? A leader who does not have a reputation based, first and foremost, in honesty will always have their actions and motivations questioned, because the leader's past behaviors, (meaning their track record of dealing with people), has earned them the reputation of not being trustworthy.

A leader with the perception that they cannot always be trusted means that leader is essentially, "dead man walking." The best a leader who does not have a reputation of being honest will get from their team is compliance based on positional authority, meaning their box in the organization chart. That leader will be viewed purely as a manager because of their place in the organization. While great management skills are treasures for an organization to have, people are more engaged when they know they are working for a person who has a foundation of honesty – meaning a foundation of being a great leader in addition to being a highly effective manager.

This wisdom is <u>not</u> a free pass to be rude and say whatever you want to whomever you want without consideration for understanding the impact on the receivers of the message. Being upfront and candid needs to be balanced with tact and genuine consideration and empathy for the feelings and perspectives of other people. A leader who is wonderfully candid and upfront without a genuine and outward consideration for people's feelings, sense of self-worth, and pride is pretty much just an ass. Effective leaders often need to be tough, make difficult decisions, deliver ugly news, and have conversations with people who need to do better, or maybe even find another job because they are not delivering the needed results. But all those difficult actions and conversations can be handled with honesty and delivered with clear concise candid words. Yet, the leaders can still treat those on the other end of the conversation with dignity and respect. Even if the other person has not performed or acted in a way deserving dignity and respect, the wise leader chooses to not lower him or herself down to the level of the worst amongst us. Remember the saying of not wrestling with the pig - the pig enjoys it, and you just get covered with muck.

Choose to operate with respect. Why? – because you need to be truly grateful each day when your people show up for work and give their best effort to help the team and company have a great day. If you are not genuinely and deeply grateful for your team, do everyone a favor and move on.

Honesty needs to become a pattern of consistent behavior that people will come to expect from you. They know they will get clear, concise, and specific feedback from you. People are pretty good at sniffing out a façade or someone prone to being a blustering buffoon. Your people will also know that _if_ you can tell them what is going on in the organization, you will. But, honesty and openness means you need to be upfront and tell your team that there will be times in which you cannot tell them something or tell them the whole "thing". Organizations do have a need to maintain a security and often a "need to know" on certain topics and events taking place. Building up your reputation of being trustworthy and respectful means you can say, "I can't say" when the need arises, and your team will be okay with that. They will not be thrilled with it. People will still be intensely curious and rumors will still fly and take on a life of their own because that is what human nature does. But, your team will know they have been dealt with honorably.

Openness works both ways. This means you are also open to the honest and candid feedback and responses from others. So, openness really means being OK with being vulnerable, and actually being candid about inviting and welcoming the feedback and ideas of others. Honesty can be uncomfortable because it may entail dealing with real issues head-on, but that is often the shortest route to truly getting those issues resolved. Honesty and openness is generally an equal opportunity communication protocol. This means that it is the right approach for good, bad, or just plain news. Establish your track record and reputation by communicating with the same open and candid style, no matter the message. If you are really disappointed with how a person or team performed, then be candid and honest and express that in the feedback. But similarly, if you are thrilled that the team or person delivered something great under tough conditions, then be just as open and candid and express honestly your pride and gratitude. The choice to operate with honesty, gratitude, and openness, is really about making the fundamental choice to be an ethical person at all times. The is a decision to be a person of principle, especially when dealing with the people providing value to the company – meaning your team.

The final thought on this wisdom: You are not being an honest, open, and candid leader, balanced with empathy and caring, for you. The end game of this wisdom, is so your people love working for you, and then also love working for the organization, and come in each day enthused to do great work for the team and the company.

REFLECTION:

So, just between you and yourself – how honest have you been with yourself, your team, your customer, your manager?

You must be your toughest critic and hold yourself to a standard higher than others have for you. Review your performance at the end of each day or week. Use a journal.

What was the most difficult interaction you had recently? Why was it difficult? Did you communicate from a spirit of respect for the other person?

Was there anything left unsaid because it would have been difficult to communicate? Was there anything left unsaid that would have lifted someone's spirit and communicated how valued they are?

If (or when) you fail at being honest AND STILL respectful, what caused you to choose to take the low road? What was the trigger in the situation that caused you to not to perform up to your expectations?

Create a list of the events, people or situations that caused you to respond in ways you came to regret.

2

WISDOM #2

LEADERS ARE IN CHARGE

This wisdom is the practice and discipline of accountability. So, as a leader it is your job to care for, and about others, to be accountable for your own actions, and operate with integrity. You are charged with making others better and serving others, not the other way around. You are responsible to know whom in your team maybe needs a little lift, a little appreciation, a little guidance, a little support, a little bit of genuine and honest feedback, and maybe a little bit more of a challenge. Your stakeholders, especially those whom you lead, really do want you to succeed and be a great leader. People like to follow great leaders, and people want to accomplish great things in their jobs, or else their job is a waste of time. People feel that a great leader, or whom they perceive as a great leader, will help them to do great work and be successful.

There may be a few exceptions to the thought that your people are motivated to always (or maybe ever) want to accomplish great things. Your employees will sometimes go into a funk. Everyone will experience a dip in energy and passion for their job. That is where a leader, who is in charge, accepts the accountability to recharge, re-inspire, re-motivate, and re-awaken the spirit and soul within each person. However, if with all your help and honest, but respectful, positive coaching, the person still does not want to accomplish great things for the team or organization, then help find that person another place to pursue their career. You are always accountable for communicating and maintaining the team's performance standards.

You hopefully obtained this leadership or management responsibility because you have demonstrated traits, actions, and a value system that the organization deems needed in a position of formal influence. There is a difference between being in charge and acting like you are in charge. Just saying it does not make it so. Titles give you certain levels of authority. The respect, confidence, trust, cooperation, and belief in you, granted by the people on your team, is what really puts you in charge. That is, unless your actions prove that their confidence and trust is misplaced.

A key concept is understanding the expectations of the organization in general and, specifically, your direct reports and all those who are now "reporting" up to you. Also, you need to understand the expectations of those above you. How do all these stakeholders in your leadership performance define "in charge"? You probably need to know that in very clear terms. So ask those who are stakeholders in your success. Especially ask those people who are entrusting you with their own career success. So be open and honest, add "being in charge", and just ask what someone expects. Now, here is the second most important step. Once you ask, all you do is just honestly listen.

Being "in charge" does not mean you have to make every decision. Great leaders, in kind of a paradox, demonstrate they are in charge by actually leveraging the talent in the organization by empowering the right people to know how and when to make the right decisions. Be in charge by empowering others. Empowerment increases the overall leadership capacity in the organization. Be in charge by guiding your team to have the right values, be courageous, and have confidence to help move the team forward. Empowerment is an act of leadership accountability that unleashes the tremendous potential in your people.

Being in charge means you set and control key organizational and cultural factors in your team. This means that the leader is in charge of perpetuating the right values and positive ethos at every level with every person. They are in charge by making it clear how "we" operate and treat each other, our customers, how we make decisions, and how we demonstrate accountability and personal responsibility. In other words, leaders are in charge of forming and sustaining a positive effective culture that will enable organizational success.

The most effective way leaders do this, and therefore be "in charge", is through their actions, the words they use, and whom they talk to and why they talk to them. These are all the ways a person's true values are communicated. Another paradox is that leaders demonstrate how they are in charge, or not, by their inactions, and what they do not talk about, and whom they do not talk to, or what they do not react to. What is not talked about or dealt with also speak volumes about what the leader really values. Whom you rarely, if ever, talk to, may speak volumes about where those people rank in your opinion and having value.

A litmus test on an effective leader is what he or she considers to be a big deal, or perhaps even a crisis. Leaders are not in charge when they elevate every event into a crisis. Leaders who consistently over-react to the ups and downs and daily speed bumps that happen in organizations are letting the environment be "in charge" and control them. Wise leaders know how to control the situation, rather than let the situation control them. A leader who can be in charge during the tough times is invaluable at calming the organization, yet, at the same time, can get their people to move with urgency and passion to deal effectively with the situation.

Be in charge by making time to define the future of your team, rather than just reacting to the winds of change. Be in charge by defining where your team needs to grow to continue to add value to the business, not just for today, but for where the business is heading in the future. Be in charge by not letting business changes pass by you or your team. A leader is fundamentally accountable to ensure that their team is always adding value and is aligned with where the overall business is headed. That whooshing sound you hear might be the evolving business strategy that you and your team are supposed to support, blowing by your team's capabilities to support it. Be in charge of the vision, and the achievement of that vision.

So, now that you have defined the value your team needs to provide, being in charge means you will track your team's success at providing that value. A leader who is in charge will determine the right metrics to track and manage organizational output and progress. There is validity to the axiom of, "what gets measured, gets managed". So, the effective leader, who is responsible for his/her organization providing value to the business, will determine what the very few, but very clear, metrics are that communicate how the organization is delivering on its mission. It is also far better to have three concise, brutally clear, and easily understood metrics than ten complicated metrics that are fuzzy enough that the results can be debated or misinterpreted to tell the "right" story. These clear and indisputable metrics should have buy in from the team that these are the right measuring stick. But, you are still in charge to ensure the metrics are fair, relevant, objective and clearly understandable, and published in manner to be visible to the team. Everyone needs to know the score.

The wise leader realizes that time is an asset that gets consumed regardless of your actions. Comments like, "I did not have time to..., or I ran out of time," are not the comments of a leader who is in charge. A leader who is in charge will be more honest and self-aware and state what really happened, which is "I CHOSE not to spend time on.....", or "I CHOSE to spend time on these other needs/projects/requests, etc." Each leader is basically defined by the choices he or she makes. Be in charge of your time. Be accountable for all your choices.

Leaders who are in charge do not remove every bit of stress in the organization. However, they are "in charge" to some degree of how much stress exists. No stress in an organization is a climate that deflates creativity, innovation, a desire to compete and win, and an urgency to deliver excellence to the customer. Excessive stress will burn people out. It will also cause short-sighted decisions, and may cause a cultural paranoia and defensiveness. There needs to be some degree of heat on in the organization from which the "in charge" leader can increase when needed for a true and valid important cause or project, and then decrease to celebrate success or just to give the team a chance to take a collective breath and recharge.

However, wise leaders are "fire-preventers" first, and "fire-fighters" second. Reporting to a leader who loves being the hero in a crisis can be an emotional roller coaster because the leader's addiction to the adrenaline of putting out fires can be tough to overcome, and that stress, real or manufactured, is almost always spread to that leader's direct reports.

A leader who is in charge makes others more productive. Being in charge means you remove ambiguity, i.e. "lift the fog" about what success looks like for your team, and then clears the hurdles to be successful. A leader who is in charge is not a man or woman of mystery. The wise leader will clearly state what their organization owns and will deliver, and also clearly state what is not owned. A leader with high accountability does not say "yes sir" to everything. This concept is not about being a "good soldier" and take that hill (unless, of course, you are a platoon leader and you have been ordered to, well, take that hill). In business, an accountable leader is one who is a pragmatic and clear leader who loves the people reporting to him/her. Therefore, the effective leader helps the larger organization determine how best to "take that hill" in a manner that is successful for the business in terms of costs, time, and results.

Those challenging initiatives are also successful and valuable because it provides opportunities for the team to shine and accomplish great results. The opportunity to succeed is a pretty standard motivator and has been one of the constants across the generations in the work force. Your people, regardless of their age, really do like to win, and be given the opportunity to do something enjoyable, that is important to someone, has value to the team and can be achieved – with the right support. The leader who is in charge sets his/her team up for success.

That leader builds the "right team for the right job". The effective leader also becomes a part of that "right team" and works hard, in the trenches, to make the team successful.

The final thought on this wisdom: do not hide behind policy, processes, and rules. Own your decisions and stand behind your actions. This is not an attitude of self-righteousness. You are being a leader who is charge, not to satisfy your own ego or desire to control or micro-manage, but to lift up your team, drive great success for your organization, and to build up the leadership skills and empowerment in those people who consider you their leader. You are a leader who loves being in charge of helping your people be successful. So those people will then love that you are their leader, and respond by coming in each day to do great work for the team and the company.

REFLECTION:

Track the decisions you make during the course of a week. Are you really the right person to make that decision?   Are you missing an opportunity to elevate the leadership skills of others? Empowerment is a development activity. Who did you chose to let be in charge of something this week that helped grow their skills?

Track the conversations you have with your team. Are they for fire-fighting or fire prevention?

How did you react to the last bit of bad news or last crisis situation?

What are the "numbers" from the past week that tells the truth about how your team is performing?

What numbers would tell your boss's boss that your team is doing a great job?   Or not?

3

WISDOM #3

LEADERS ARE NOT OBLIGATED TO PERPETUATE FOOLISHNESS

In reality, leaders are expected to <u>stop</u> foolishness when it is discovered. This is the practice and discipline of being a courageous leader. This is another chapter where the underlying theme is courage to do the right thing, and being an action and <u>results-oriented</u> leader. So, ultimately this is about where the leader sets the bar for expectations for the organization to be a smart, pragmatic, and have a focus on results.

Many times leaders and managers are focused on what to start doing, the next big thing, the next cure-all process change or the next program from the latest consultant. However, the wise leader takes the time to ponder the opposite of focusing on the "new", by pondering the "old" or the "current". They think about, "addition through subtraction". Look for the gains your organization can make just by stopping the organization from doing stupid stuff. Such as wasteful activities, processes that no longer add value, work product that no one uses and the documents being produced that will never be read.

Consider the classic example of organizational foolishness – rudderless meetings! Those are the meetings that do not, and will not, result in actions taken or decisions made. Meetings often had a good reason to exist at some point, but usually degrade over time as their mission and purpose no longer exists. The wise leader effectively uses meetings, and really all forms of communication and interaction, to reinforce or at least remind all the participants of the values of the organization and his/her leadership team. Also, how those meetings are run – with a meaningful purpose, with open, productive and inclusive dialogue, and with an appropriate conclusions, decisions, and/or actions assigned. Wise leaders practicing this discipline will be able to complete the sentence – "that was a great meeting because". If that sentence is difficult to complete, then that might be an opportunity to stop some foolishness. However, even the above taken to an extreme, is foolish. Meetings should always be efficient, but sometimes the value in the meeting was from the personal interaction the leader had with members of his/her organization. Any meeting is an opportunity to express your values and build relationships. Remember, if you are following these leadership wisdoms, you may be developing a reputation as a leader that people want to be exposed to in order to learn. From Wisdom #2, we know that people really want to be led by great leaders. So, do not perpetuate the foolishness of <u>not choosing</u> to make the time to interact with your organization. Interact with your team and let your values be known throughout the land!

Being in charge often means you will need to kill some ingrained beliefs or organizational habits. People, by their nature, take comfort in the tried and true, the tools and processes that have served them well and helped them be successful for quite some time. This learned and now, ingrained, tendency to stick with the "present" has been defined as <u>organizational inertia</u>.   As business, the marketplace, customers, and all those factors that impact an organization evolve, organizational inertia will cause organization to be too slow to react and evolve along with their environments to remain competitive. So, effective leaders challenge the status quo. As a leader, first don't allow your organization to keep doing silly stuff out of habit. However, this takes an ability for the leader to be able to develop an internal antenna to help detect low value, or even counter-productive activities. Usually hearing people say, "we have always done it that way" might be a sign that something may need to be examined.

There is a tale of a husband asking his wife why she always cut an inch off the end of the roast before cooking it. She replied that her mother just did it that way. So, she asked her mother why she did that. Her reply was that was because her mother did that also. So, she asked her grandmother. Grandma said her roasting pan was too small and was not large enough for the roast she got from the butcher. So, she had to cut off an inch or so to have it fit in the pan. Therefore, a restriction and subsequent "work around" that was valid many years ago, survived generations when the restriction, (pan size) had long gone away.

Seek to understand the "why" – meaning where is the business value derived from a process, tool, or decision. Use the <u>Five Whys</u> approach to getting to the root of why something is being done. The Five Whys technique seeks to dive deeper into an issue to uncover root causes or determine where the true business value is derived from a process. Five Whys was first used by Toyota to do process improvement and defect analysis on its automobile parts manufacturing processes.

The technique is quite simple. Just ask your first question on the topic, and then ask "why" (or why do we do that, or why does that happen, etc.), to the answer you are given. The theory was that it generally took 5 iterations of asking why to get to what is really the root cause or reason why something is done. If the answer to any of the "whys" is "I don't know", that may be a sign that the process or solution should be challenged. Be in charge, and ask why to get closer to the heart of the issue. Use the Five Whys with an open mind, a learner's mind, and then shut up, and listen with an open mind, a mind truly and honestly set on "learn" mode. You will be amazed at what you can learn when that is really your honest objective.

The final thought on this wisdom: have the courage to perpetuate the value of doing what makes sense and what is right. Making "sense" and doing what is "right" rarely conflict. Good people treasure doing what is right, and not doing things that are silly, wasteful, or just dumb because doing things that are low value is not the foundation for a great career. Be a leader who makes people proud to call you their leader because it just makes sense, and that results in people who come in each day to do great work for the team and the company.

REFLECTION:

Ask yourself each week, what meetings were a waste of time?

What actions did the team take this week that you are not sure why it is done that way?

What changes do you need to deploy that will go against the flow of the current organizational inertia?

Is your team producing anything that no one consumes and likely never will?

4

WISDOM #4

LEADERS MUST CHOOSE WHICH PROBLEM(S) TO LIVE WITH

There are very few perfect solutions – ever. This wisdom is the practice and discipline of leading by "staying in the moment". Life in any organization is generally messy and revolves around fixing problems each and every day. Honest leaders acknowledge that fact, accept it, and choose to be in charge of dealing with problems in a positive manner. Effective leaders need to develop their skills and behaviors that support being comfortable with being uncomfortable. Otherwise, you will go insane and drive everyone around you nuts in the process.

All decisions and actions have consequences. In the reality of life in an organization, there are almost always some negative consequences, and the probability that the actions you take will indeed cause an "uh oh" moment. This includes the negative consequences you could and should likely see coming (and can consider and possibly mitigate), and those that completely blindside you. Get used to life being messy, and move on.

Realize that you are expected, and paid, to help your organization be successful. Rarely, even in the short-term, will organizational success be accomplished by <u>inactions</u> on the part of its leaders. Effective leaders need to be action-oriented, and yet, know that they may often be asked to make decisions that are based on imperfect or incomplete information. Those decision are often built upon "iffy" assumptions made by themselves or others and being communicated to the leader through the personal bias and filters of the people involved. With all those factors, count your blessings when a decision or action actually works as planned. You beat the odds!

Skilled and wise leaders understand that not all the actions they take need to be dramatic. In fact, strong leaders seek to take actions, that are more often than not, subtle in nature, and purposely lack drama or flair. One of the laws of Newtonian physics applies to leadership and a leader's actions. Newton's third law states that for every action there is an equal and opposite reaction. Big dramatic actions can also go badly in big and dramatic ways. So, sometimes the boring decision can be a good thing. However, it is true that every so often an organization or team needs to have an action that is dramatic to kick it into a higher gear of performance. Collins and Porras introduced the concept of BHAGS – big hairy audacious goals, to be catalysts to introduce a new culture or way of thinking into an organization. BHAGS are a great tool, and like any great tool, there is a time and a situation where that tool may be an option. Big tools should be used for big problems, not the daily speed bumps of life. Match the intensity of your actions to the urgency or seriousness of the problem. Keep little issues little. Keep mole hills as mole hills. Life is better when the road only has little bumps and gentle curves.

Leaders need to realize they will be looked to constantly to make decisions, give opinions and advice on the daily happenings that take place during the ebb and flow of life. That really is part of the paradigm of being a leader – see principle #2 (leaders are in charge). So, leaders need to stay in touch with life within their organizations. Leaders stay in touch by turning the tables, so to speak, on this paradigm and using the empowerment, hopefully, that you have been building in your organization. Effective leaders stay in touch with their organizations by making it a point to ask for opinions, and ask for advice from the right people on the team. Build up the problem-solving capability in the organization by involving your team in hurdles facing the enterprise.

Your decisions sometimes communicate trust or, lack of trust, in others. How you assess risk, and whom you involve in your decisions communicates trust and respect. However, this is not about delegating the decision-making. You are the leader, you are in charge, so don't waffle or push the decisions to others to escape the accountability for the decision. Also, not making a decision or taking action, is in reality a decision and an action. Come to accept the reality that you will make decisions that will not turn out well, and many that will be questioned by the Monday morning quarterbacks in the organization. That's life, accept it, let it go, move on.

As mentioned above, you need to accept that your decision-making processes are not perfect, and rarely built upon perfect information. So, what you can control is how you analyze your options. This means you need always to examine the problem and your options through the lens of your values and the organization's. These values need to be the bright beacons lighting your way. The last point assumes your organization's values are positive, ethical, and based on moral principles. Because, if they are not, an organization will implode from the weight of the toxic culture built upon poor values.

Okay, so I think you have now reached the most confusing paragraph in this little book. I am going to introduce my twist on the concepts of good, bad, right, and wrong, in terms of the quality of your decisions. There is a difference between good and bad decisions and right and wrong decisions. "Good and bad" is different from "right and wrong". The right decision can have bad results. The actions you take, via the decisions you make and don't make, reflect your values and are powerful influences in your organization. Decisions you make that are not aligned with your organization's leadership values, are WRONG decisions, whether or not those decisions had <u>good</u> results. On the flip side, decisions you make that are aligned with your organization's leadership values, are the RIGHT decisions, whether or not those decisions had <u>good</u> or <u>bad</u> results. The key is that you consciously consider those values and can cite the values you considered on the path to taking the action you did. Easy right? Well, not so fast. Because, to make it even more complicated, an organization's value system will, at times, have specific values that conflict with other values. Therefore, as a leader, you will often have to choose the values that are more important or relevant to the problem you are needing to solve.

It takes practice and self-control to slow down your decision-making process to give yourself the time truly consider the relevant values to the issue, and make the right decision. Now – a note of caution – making the right decision will, at times, be difficult and not without personal risk to your career. Swaying to the organizational winds or the loudest voice is easy.

Standing up for the right values – yours and the organizations can, at a minimum, be uncomfortable, and potentially, career limiting. Your options for choosing which problem to live with is rarely between two "happy" solutions. The reality of life is often not so sweet.

Often wisdom #2 – being in charge gets construed with being a fast, decisive, always-has-the-answer kind of person. Being in charge means you have the courage to stand for doing things right, rather than fast. Give yourself the space and time to make the right decisions and fix the problem as best you can. Realize that perfection is often a foolish pursuit – "the perfect is the enemy of the good" (Voltaire).

Organizations and teams can be and stay successful when built upon a track record of consistently "right" decisions, day after day, month after month, year after year. As you practice keeping the organizational and your personal values front and center to your thinking, you will get faster and more efficient at the application of those values to solving the problems and making the decisions that confront you on a daily basis. Don't forget, your practice needs to be consistent - day after day, month after month, and year after year. Most organizational cultures seem to reward speedy actions over thoughtful value-based decision-making processes and behaviors. So, as mentioned above, you may be swimming against the current when you chose to solve problems by letting the right values guide you. So, practice, as the current is likely to be strong and the sharks are circling.

Now, as was mentioned above, you are making tough choices about what problems and negative consequences you are choosing to accept. However, also as mentioned above,

YOU WILL BE BLINDSIDED by a decision you make, and that is when it gets interesting. Your values are also reflected in how you react when the decision did not work out, and often it is your stronger more deeply held personal values that rise to the surface when something hits the fan. So, really think before you open your mouth and express your emotions.

Now, this is not saying not to be emotional in your response to a curve ball being thrown your way. Your people want to see that you care, were surprised, perplexed, disappointed or frustrated. However, make sure your response and emotions target the issue, process, or problem, not the people who perhaps did their absolute best and tried hard, but things just did not work out. Always appreciate the effort, but results do matter – a lot.

Notice I did not include anger in the list of emotions to be displayed. Anger does have a place in an organization, but only in very specific and hopefully quite rare "places". However, an organization built upon "angry" or negative leaders will not succeed. The competition for talent is so great that the top talent will gravitate towards positive and optimistic cultures and leadership values. You can be angry with yourself for how you failed to correctly analyze the situation. You can be angry with the immaturity of certain organizational processes that let you down. But, really think it through before you get angry with people who have tried their best.

However, people who are not doing their best and appear not to really want to do their best, are a disappointment and need to be dealt with – but not with anger. Remember, leaders are in charge. Anger with people may be the right response when their actions put people's health and well-being at risk.

However, leaders are also just ordinary imperfect people. So, you will get mad because some situation or people just pushed all the buttons and caused you to lose control and no longer be in control for your emotions, even if only for a few minutes. Leaders who are honest and in charge will recognize their mistake and do the honest thing – apologize, commit to work to get better, and move on.

The final thought on this wisdom: you will <u>not</u> always make everything perfect or maybe even really good. Any organization faces an environment/world that may not really care if it survives. So, now you are an honest leader who is in charge, trying to instill a sense of what is right, by dealing with the curve balls being thrown at you and the team. Realize perfection is not necessarily the goal. Your legacy should be in creating engaged teams. Passionate teams who can roll with the punches, remain positive, and remain dedicated to the team to achieve the best results possible with the cards they are dealt. Engaged teams have energized and passionate people who come in each day to do great work for the team and the company.

REFLECTION:

Review the decisions you've made during the day or week and write down the values communicated in those decisions. Were those the right values?

Did you demonstrate the value of forgiveness that you and your team are all just human and will likely have made mistakes during the week?

5

WISDOM #5

RUN THE COMPANY (I.E. YOUR TEAM) SO THE BEST PEOPLE LOVE IT

Unless of course you are managing a prison chain gang, in reality, you have an entirely volunteer work force making up your organization. So, in reality, your people volunteer again and again each day when they show up for work. So, this wisdom of creating emotional bonds of trust and respect with all your volunteers – and especially your stars. This wisdom is not about creating a caste system or two sets of standards – for "stars" and "non-stars", because "non-stars" are perhaps just "stars-in-waiting". They just need the experience, skills, opportunity, and sincere support from you to be able to shine. But, this wisdom is also definitely not about lowering your expectations and standards for the lowest performing people in the organization. Your expectations need to align with the results the organization needs to your team to deliver.

An effective and wise leader sets the values and expectations for the organization that will excite, motivate, build loyalty, and create engagement for everyone in the organization. Excitement and engagement can be, and is usually, spread from team member to team member. Peers influence peers and, everybody usually knows who the top performers are and why. Your top performers are key influencers to others in the organization. However, it is also the nature of organizations that not everyone is a top performer. The "bell curve" is a one way to view the talent within an organization. A few of your folks are top performers. A solid majority are good performers. However, a few people have checked out or are just not fit for the skills needed, values, and productivity needed. The good, solid, come-in-everyday, work hard and deliver good results are also important to keep engaged because this may be where a majority of your production is coming from. The wise leader lets these people know they are also truly valued and appreciated. Maybe even more so, because it may be that source of encouragement that moves the needle for these people to the higher levels of motivation and engagement - to become more star-like.

But there is the other end of the bell curve of employees and, like all your actions as a leader, how you deal with people issues communicates your values. This is where the role of leader gets tough, but remember wisdom #2 – you are in charge. A leader's tolerance for people who are not giving their best and not producing the needed results gives clear signals to everyone of exactly how high or low the expectations bar has been set. There is rarely a one-size-fits-all answer for performance issues because everyone on your team is a unique individual. The malcontents are easy to address. Poisonous attitudes left to fester and spread like a fungus need to be removed quickly. You probably owe it to the person to seek to understand the "why" behind attitude – maybe, maybe not. But an honest conversation that seeks to peel away the layers to uncover the real issue, might be all that is needed. So ask, then really listen.

Clarify your understanding, and then state your concerns and requirements for the person's performance. Communicate why improved performance is important, the timeline to show improvement (like right now), and the consequences for <u>not choosing</u> to change and meet the requirements of your organization and the values you fully intend to uphold for the benefit of everyone.

The tougher conversations are with those who have a good heart, work hard, and are nice people, but just do not have the experience or skills needed to be productive member of the team. The wise leader will first ask him/herself how this situation came to pass and face this issue with compassion. Then determine what can be done to elevate the skills and abilities of this person to be a functional member of the team, and how much time can be afforded for this growth. Some can be turned around, but not all. But, even your best people will appreciate the respect and honor you show to those struggling to do a good job or those dealing with personal issues that are causing their attitude and performance to suffer. Paraphrasing Robert Greenleaf from his wonderful book Servant Leadership: anyone could lead perfect people - if there were any. Many good people are cannot be effective leaders because they cannot work with and through the flawed people that make up the work place. Remember, everyone is flawed, even you.

The salary, benefits, and working conditions are really just the price of entry for people to stay in their jobs. For the most part, those factors are just based on money. Pretty much any company can compete for talent based on money, if they choose to. But, the wise leader knows that people stay because the "price of entry" is fair, AND the organization has a value-added quality, kind of a secret sauce that keeps people continuing to show up every day, to "volunteer" once more to provide great work. Wise and empowering leaders, who demonstrate day in and day out that they are thrilled that he/she has these great people on the team, goes a long way towards creating this secret sauce.

The wise leader, knowing that the competition for talent is intense, will know who their stars are. They will also know why their stars are volunteering every day to come in and work for you and the company. You need to have a really good idea of what is important to them, what they like about the organization, what motivates, what de-motivates, and know why they will stay. And, most importantly, why they might leave.

Let your stars know you consider them stars because that is what honest and candid leaders do. Often the only time people hear they will be missed and were important to the company is during their exit interview. That's really kind of pathetic. If that happens, it may be the leader that needs to be replaced. The greatest influence on employee retention is the employee's immediate supervisor. That does not mean coddle your stars. Everyone needs to pull their weight respective to their abilities and be a contributor to the team. No special treatment for the stars, just special opportunities that their great performance has earned them. Even the top performers need to do things people do not like doing, but need to be done, be tolerated and completed well.

A fairly easy way to build up trusting relationships is simply by genuinely and consistently listening to your people – stars and non-stars. So look for ways to have a reason to listen. Asking people for their opinion, feedback, solutions, suggestions for lunch, how to celebrate an accomplishment, etc.

all communicate that a leader thinks that person is important and is valued because you wanted to hear from them. Let people solve their own problems or, even better, solve your problems, and tell you how they did that. Ask away, and then shut up and listen. Ask for more opinions, engage in "what ifs". But, ask and listen, and always say thanks for the input, opinion, and perspective. Show you are grateful that your people are thinking, because truly "thinking" means they care. Seeing people who truly care about the success of the team, is usually a characteristic of a highly effective and successful team.

The final thought on this wisdom: you are nothing without the people on your team. There are not many more powerful reputations to have then to be as a leader known for developing superstars and creating more leaders to go out into the organization to do great things in their own right. Let your legacy be the quantity of great people you have helped develop. The people who continue to come in each day to do great work for the team and the company because you instilled the values, passion, and pride within them.

REFLECTIONS:

Every leader should know the following:

Who are your best people?

Why are they your stars?

Why do they stay with you or the company?

Why would they leave?

Who will be your stars in three years?

Do they know you feel that way about them?

6

WISDOM #6

SIT IN THE GRANDSTAND. GET THE RIGHT PERSPECTIVES ON THE SITUATION

This is the wisdom of being an inclusive leader. Think about how a baseball game can look different and be experienced differently based on where you are sitting. Three rows behind home plate is a different view and experience than the upper deck in the right field corner. So, this is about including the people with different perspectives in the decisions and actions that will have an impact on the organization, team, project, or business. You include others specifically because they have different perspectives than you and perhaps anyone else on the team. Those differences are invaluable.

Now, in the spirit of full disclosure, this is a wisdom that I really "re-examined" and "refreshed" from the original wording for the purposes of this book. This wisdom was originally written as "Get all the liars in the same room". I felt that came across a bit harsh and did not really send the right message of treating people with honor and respect. The underlying intent of the original wisdom was to get everyone's version of the truth from the people who have a relevant opinion on the issue. So, I morphed this wisdom to be stated in a positive tone about realizing that value can be found in everyone's perspective.

Organizations are not a democracy. Not everyone is needed or should be included in every action or decision to be made, and that who is included may be different depending on the situation. So, who are the right people to include? Think about including those who have the view of the customer/user, those who will be impacted by any actions taken and certainly those with a technical or process expertise that will be relevant. However, keep the number manageable, probably in the single digits so actions can be taken quickly without becoming a session of Congress. Also, let people know that while their opinion is valued, depending on the nature of the decision, you are accountable for making the final decision.

This wisdom is about how you communicate to people that you value them by exploring their opinions, and truly working to understand what is behind their perspectives. Inclusion in the decision making process can also be a valuable development activity for individuals in the organization, especially those that you may be targeting for future leadership roles, or whom may be new to leadership roles. This is also a way to ensure that your direct reports get reinforcement on the leadership values you want to perpetuate to all levels. One of those values should be humility. Which means you realize and truly know that you are really not omnipotent – and never will be, so that is why you are asking for help.

Involving others does not mean paralysis by analysis or falling into groupthink. Nor does it mean creating scapegoats to have in case the situation takes a negative turn i.e. "well, that was what the team recommended". This wisdom is about leveraging all the knowledge, skills, and experience you have helped bring into the team to help you be better informed and make better decisions. But, you still own that decision.

Peter Senge, in his book, The Fifth Discipline, explored how people, and leaders are people too, move through a decision-making process using a tool put forth by organizational psychologist Chris Argyris called the Ladder of Inference. To generalize, the Ladder of Inference says we take actions after moving up this ladder from the <u>facts</u> of the event to how we filter and <u>interpret</u> the facts. Our value system, past experiences, biases, and judgement all influence how our brain processes events and creates our version of the truth. Below is a brief description of this concept.

The Ladder of Inference:

o　**The First (bottom) Rung** – It all starts with an observable event or situation. This is what the camera would have seen. So, **we see or hear something**, and then all the next rungs of the Ladder of Inference come into play and influence the action we will take.

o　We then **accept & filter data** from the event or situation to focus on, or weigh as more important than other data, and we usually select or emphasize data that more aligns with our, "view of the world". See the concept of confirmation bias on the next page.

o　We **add meaning** to the events we observe and the data we chose based on our personal or cultural bias.

o   We **make assumptions,** whether we know it or not, – based on the meaning we added in the previous rung.

o   We next **draw conclusions** to make sense of it all and speed up our analysis processes, because that is what our brains like to do for our survival – help us make sense of things for our own protection.

o   We **create our system of beliefs and values** over our lifetime of experiences, formed by our observations of the world that we have come to accept as valid, true, or comforting to us.

o   **Top Rung** – We then **take an action based on our beliefs and values**, perhaps, <u>in spite of the data</u> we actually saw that triggered our action or decision.

You will find that many people can go from the bottom rung (what actually happened) to the top rung and take an action, express an opinion, or make a decision in a split second. As you are scratching your head wondering how they got from the event (point A) to what seems to be an odd conclusion (point B), keep in mind your conclusion on their conclusion went up the same ladder. You also travel the Ladder of Inference.

The wise leader understands and accepts the inaccuracies and limitations of even their own stellar intelligence. A widely held psychological phenomenon is the concept/reality of the "confirmation bias". This means that even the wisest of leaders will have a natural tendency to accept or favor information or data that validates their current set of beliefs and choose to ignore or shoot down data that runs counter to their own opinions and beliefs. So, "sitting in the grandstand" and soliciting the perspectives of others is a vital for the wise leader.

But, the truly courageous leader makes a point to take a giant step beyond soliciting from the like-minded people on the team. The wise leader will actively seek out the perspective of those who often run counter to his/her opinions and beliefs. There is little value, true learning, or wisdom to be gained by only asking those who will agree with you. The value is getting the perspective of the contrarians in the organizations, or those who may really have a fresh perspective.

The wisdom-seeking leader explores the values behind those perspectives, because that is how the leader learns about their people. Are the correct values being used to guide the action or decision being taken? Do those values align or at least do not contradict the values that you as a leader want to perpetuate in the organization? As mentioned in previous chapters, all of a leader's actions and inactions communicate the values that are guiding the leader. Being an inclusive leader for important decisions or guidance from others is a powerful action that does two things. Being included on key issues communicates trust and value to your people. Also, your people will know when they are being asked to weigh in on something of consequence or not. So, make it matter.

But, who are the "right" people? What is the impact being felt by all the stakeholders? Which stakeholders are the key ones to listen to or satisfy? Which ones are closest to the end customer, or revenue, or whatever business goal is in play? Who really has to live with the consequences of the actions being taken? All of these are questions that could help identify the "right" people.

Now it is one thing to ask for perspectives and opinions, and quite another to *actually listen* and truly use the perspectives of others to influence you and the actions you take. It's easy to just ask, but tough, and maybe courageous, to actually allow yourself to be changed because of those perspectives. The wise leader seeks opportunities to change and grow by being open to the influence of the smart people in the organization.

The final thought on this wisdom: **you are not, or rarely, going to be the smartest kid in the class.** Start off each day repeating that last sentence. Put it on a post-it note. Make it your screen saver. Therefore, be actively open and engage the smart, talented people you have worked hard, and with love, to build up and unleash into the organization. I think a truism that spans the generations is that people really want to matter. Use the greatness you have built (or perhaps are working to build) in your team. Those people will then come in each day to do great work for the team and the company because they feel truly valued and that they matter.

REFLECTION:

Whom did I ask for advice today or this week?

Whom did I include in the decisions I made this week?

Whom did I exclude? And why?

Why am I a better leader than I was a week/month/year ago?

7

WISDOM #7

RUN YOUR BUSINESS/TEAM/PROJECT LIKE IT'S YOUR COMPANY

Be all in. Leaders who are just "OK" leaders like to operate with a safety net for their own career self-preservation. This wisdom is about operating from a perspective of being on offense rather than on defense for the success of your organization. Operate from the position of being a courageous leader who ties their personal career success to the success of the company, their team, organization, and/or project. Courageous and great leaders are "all in".

I used the clarifier of "career" success for a reason. Wise leaders also realize, for their own well-being, their success in life, as an accomplished person, is not solely defined by their jobs. They realize the need to maintain the ability to balance the work/non-work aspects of their lives. They prioritize their own family, physical/mental/spiritual health, and service to a greater good above "the job". This balanced approach to life gives them the ability to be a positive role model to their teams. But, wise leaders know that when they are "on the job" they owe it to their teams and the company to focus and give their best thinking and dedication to the success of the enterprise. Meaning, when they are working, they are "all in".

People are generally perceptive at detecting leaders who have the habit and talent of hedging their bets when it comes to being accountable for the results of their organization. When the team knows their leaders are positioning themselves to have a coat of Teflon, it drastically changes their emotional commitment as well. The team will mirror their leader and operate from a position of defense and of self-preservation. So, they spend a certain amount of time and energy first seeking to protect themselves instead of contributing their energy and best focused thinking on the success of the team, project, organization or company. People know when their leaders have not jumped into the deep end of the pool i.e. are not really "all in". So therefore, they judge the culture to be somewhat less than safe for themselves and their career security. People will then act rationally and take steps to protect themselves, as they see their leader doing. They are just following their leader. So, then no one in the organization is really "all in". Then the executives wonder why the organization is not innovative, and is slow to respond to the changes in the market or environment in which they must compete. That culture changes with leaders who have the courage to be "all in".

This is also about accountability for the results of your organization. Great leaders have the mindset that whatever the organization is expecting them to deliver is smack dab in the middle of their plate. They tie their personal career success to the success of those expected deliverables. Highly accountable leaders also set the bar for themselves higher than anyone else will. They also know, that every so often, they will fail – because the deliverables did not measure up to expectations.

But, "fail" is not always a four-letter word. Mistakes will happen. Results will fall short. Strategies and tactics will miss the target. People will disappoint. Because people, including the wise leaders, as pointed out by Robert Greenleaf, will always be imperfect. We are all flawed. But that does not lessen the need for leaders to focus and have a passion for their teams, organizations, and especially the people under their stewardship to become great. Leaders need to be "all in". A leader being passionate about the success of the organization and each individual is one of those leadership values that gets reinforced frequently, especially when the road gets rocky.

Money is one of the clearest way to communicate organizational values. This is the big dollar amounts – like what gets funded in various budgets. Like funds for training, big and little perks, and "thank you's". During those times those budgets are pretty much at zero, you may need to say thanks on your own. Take out your own credit card. Is something important enough that you would pay for it? Often, companies manage expenses for relatively low-cost team events, like an occasional lunch or something to celebrate even a small victory or accomplishment. Buy the occasional cookies, bagels, pizza, even though you may not get reimbursed by the company. Spending a few bucks for expressing gratitude returns many times the cost in terms of employee morale. In addition, it allows you to demonstrate your values through your actions. Now – should you put yourself into debt through this action? Probably not. Should you pay for something expressly forbidden, or that runs contrary to company policy? That's probably not wise. But, FTD Florists had the slogan, "say it with flowers". Sometimes you need to say it with pizza, or cookies, or bagels, or donuts.

Do you communicate your budget to your team, or at least to your direct reports? Letting people know where the fences are relative to how much your organization has to spend to support itself is part of being upfront, honest, and candid. Especially in times when your budgets are under pressure to cut back a little or a lot. However, wise leaders also expand their definition of what is in their budget to include more than just financial currency. You also have a currency that is based in time and words. Wise leaders actively budget their time to ensure that their time is truly well spent. To your team, how you spend your time is a very tangible sign of what, and whom, you really value. Ensure you spend your time well by making the rounds to your team, or giving them a call if they are remote. Also, ensure you spend your "words" wisely. A well-timed and sincere "thank you" can have a tremendous return on investment. As can just a bit of small talk, such as asking about someone's project, or maybe even their kids. Be all in by also sincerely paying attention to your people, every day.

The final thought on this wisdom: be a committed leader. Experience the pain when things do not go well, or are not going well. Ride the high tide with your team when things are clicking on all cylinders. Be accountable for the results and celebrate the wins and learn from the losses. Build a team of people who come in each day to do great work for the team and the company because they know their leader is with them every step of the way – in good times and, especially, the bad times.

REFLECTION:

How have I said thanks this week? And to whom?

What did not work so well this past week? How did I react? What was I passionate about this past week?

Did I make the time to have a conversation with everyone on my team? Who did I not talk to this past week?

8

WISDOM #8

NO SECOND CHANCE TO MAKE A FIRST IMPRESSION

However, <u>you are always making an impression</u>. Every interaction, conversation, joke in the elevator, and rolling of your eyes leaves an impression. Think first, then act. This is the wisdom of being a self-aware leader, and a leader who actively seeks to maintain perspective.

All your actions and words are subject to interpretation. All those on the receiving end of your messages are filtering your actions through their own personal set of filters of how they view the world <u>and you</u>. See the Ladder of Inference described in Chapter 6. The odds of delivering your intended message with 100% accuracy to all the receivers is pretty low because your listeners are traveling up their own Ladder of Inference as they hear your words. The intent of your message at a simplistic level has two parts: what you want people to hear and understand, and then what you DO NOT want them to hear, understand, and perceive. Both parts are influenced by trust.

If you have continued to work at getting to know your team, you will have likely built up positive and trusting relationships.

When you have trusting relationships, you can then be open to feedback from others. The open leader can have the people they trust coach them on how their message through their actions and words may actually be perceived. This simple act of asking for coaching (or an opinion) from your people is also an act that communicates trust and strengthens the level of empowerment they feel they have. Actively seek feedback. Actively fine-tune your antenna of how you are coming across to others.

This wisdom is also about validating and staying true to your "brand" as leader. Especially with regards to how your message is aligning with the values you verbalize and the expectations you have set. Your brand evolves with each interaction you have with your people, customers, or anyone in the organization. So, your brand is not established as 100% complete with the first impressions you have made with each of your stakeholders. Your brand, as it relates to your values, is molded and remolded, reinforced or eroded, each and every day. Think first, then act.

There is no more important time to be aware of the true values you are communicating as when there is a problem – big or little. It is the judgement, tone, decision-making, and treatment of people that are often magnified and scrutinized even more when there is a problem, of any size or criticality. Actually, it's the small problem where the unwise leader creates some undesirable impressions, because of their tendency to over-react and treat relatively minor issues as the end of Western civilization if not corrected ASAP! Think first, then act! When the heat is really on, think first and then rethink, and then act. People's senses are heightened when a problem arises. Probably part of our "fight or flight" human nature when something bad happens. So, your actions will be "over-interpreted" by your team. Now this is not telling you to take your sweet time about making the call, giving direction, and making assignments. When there is a problem, especially a big one, you do need to move with urgency. But balance that urgency with a sense of perspective, calmness, and control.

Your people are looking to you to be the captain of the ship, and lead from the front with a demeanor of confidence and belief that they can get through this event, which may be often very difficult to do. Perspective is often a key, but difficult, attribute to maintain. Let little problems remain little. Life is messy. Things go wrong or astray pretty much every day. People are imperfect, and will make mistakes that may cost your business customers, revenue, or diminish the quality of product or services you deliver. People may do things that may make you angry, to the point where you want to really display that emotion. At times, anger is an appropriate response. However, maintain perspective when playing the "anger" card. Because if you play it too often, and for what is perceived as the trivial, your often-displayed anger just modifies your leadership brand that you cannot maintain control in even the smallest of issues. Anger is a card played rarely and perhaps only in circumstances that are truly dire. Will someone die or get injured? Will the business be shut down? Will someone go to jail? Will the sun not come up in the East tomorrow? Take a breath and ask yourself if blowing a gasket is really the optimal choice to make.

Johnson & Johnson is one of the most trusted brands in the world, and yet, that company experienced one of the most devastating events in the history of over-the-counter health care products in 1982 when Tylenol was laced with cyanide in Chicago. But J&J (at least to the outside world) reacted with leadership and urgency and a genuine concern for their customers by removing all Tylenol from all stores until the cause was determined. Those actions reinforced the J&J brand as a highly responsible company with a perspective of putting the health and safety of its customers before profits.

Your brand is also being modified by how you react to conflict and disagreements in the normal course of interactions in business. Your use of position power with your team or peers in a manner that allows you to "win" or get your way, just because you can, communicates your true values. All your actions and inactions, words spoken and how they are spoken, or not spoken reinforces your values, which is the essentially the foundation of your brand. Your actions and words are always being judged. Those doing the judging will likely all have different criteria by which they are judging you and determining your brand to them (based on their own Ladder of Inference). Sounds kind of hopeless to ever have the brand you want to with everyone. Yep, it probably is. You can't please everybody. So, this is where you accept that you are leading by the values you treasure, and you are creating a leadership brand, of which, you can truly be proud.

I mentioned in Wisdom #4 that an organization built upon values that are based on socially and morally unethical principles will eventually create a toxic culture that would drive that organization to failure. I am also sure that without too much effort you can find exceptions to my above statement. There are exceptions to every rule. But, I will always place my bets on the organization that intentionally defines and announces to the world the positive values by which it will choose to operate. The great organizations will also take the next step and formally define those values to everyone as its leadership brand.

Successful and great organizations generally have defined values that put their stake in the ground about how they desire to run their company in the areas of people, product, and profit. Non-profits usually substitute "service" for product, and "contribution" for profit. Positive and socially responsible values that guide leaders and help organizations thrive generally have these themes:

o Choosing to treat their people ethically with a respect and generosity that communicates that they are truly valued for the talented human beings that they are.

o Operating from a position of always seeking to provide value to the marketplace. Which usually translates into being a profitable company that rewards the investment and risk taking of the owners and stakeholders of the company.

o Providing great products and services to the marketplace or whomever is the consumer of their products or services. This can include valuing the safety, innovation, reliability, quality, durability, etc. of their products or services.

o Being a well-respected member of whatever community in which the organization operates. This includes operating with a high degree of integrity and stewardship towards the larger community in which it exists.

The final thought on this wisdom: you are always reinforcing the true values you hold dear to guide you. Check yourself early and often to ensure the right values are really driving your actions and inactions. Know that your consistent and positive values will motivate people to come in each day to do great work for the team and the company because they know what to expect from you – and they love it.

REFLECTION:

Think back to a significant decision you made this week. Deconstruct the steps and thinking you went through to get to the choice you made. Write down how you would defend that decision. What were the factors that influenced you?

What were the values you exhibited in the choice you made?

What values did you choose to ignore?

What did you do this past week that was a conscious action intended to set an example or be a role model for others?

9

WISDOM #9

BAD NEWS, UNLIKE WINE AND CHEESE, DOES NOT GET BETTER WITH AGE

See snake, kill snake. Effective leaders do things. Effective leaders generally do the right things in a timely manner. They are action-oriented and results focused. Never is the expectation higher, and the leader's actions more scrutinized then when the bad stuff happens. Your mettle as a leader is put to the test when you have to deal with negative events. It is easy to be a good leader when everything is rosy. But, when problems arise, typically people may be caught off guard, because it messes with their routine and perception of what is normal, and therefore their sense of personal security. People want a leader to be effective at righting the ship, or leading the team through the mine field. People want everything to be OK and back to whatever is defined as normal, so they can feel comfortable and safe again.

This behavior ties back to Wisdom # 4 on dealing with the imperfect. However, this is not necessarily about being fast to make a decision. This is about urgency and playing the odds, not shooting from the hip. Wise leaders still gather the facts, consult with the right people in the organization (and/or outside of the organization), and determine the options and consequences. However, it is that thinking through the consequences of an action that many leaders skip. Often they miss seeing how an option or decision may play out, because they do not engage the brains of the smart people to get perspectives other than their own. Wise leaders ask the negative questions. They ask "Why will this option fail miserably?" Negative questions, that help leaders explore the "dark side" of a decision, are not asked often enough because that forces the leader to admit there is a possibility this decision could backfire. Then, (gasp), the leader may have been wrong and made a mistake, and, therefore, is really just human after all.

Move with urgency. Allowing problems to linger sends a clear message about your true values. So, problems can be like time bombs, for which you should make an assessment of how much time is on the clock. For example, if you see an employee clearly exhibiting behaviors that are way out of bounds for being acceptable, legal, or safe for the workplace, the clock on that problem may be quite short. Assuming there are not some amazing extenuating circumstances, remove that person from the workplace and move on. The longer you take means that, in reality, the more you are truly accepting the lower or incorrect performance as a standard. You set bar lower for everyone. Wise leaders also realize the power of gravity to the bar of expectations. It's easy to lower the bar, but tough to raise it; especially if performing to the low expectations is rewarded as much as the higher expectations.

So, let me explain how "see snake, kill snake" is a good way to approach, for leaders who are in charge, to resolve the problems reaching up to bite them in the, well, somewhere.

"See Snake, Kill Snake" came from a talk and an article in Fortune Magazine from Ross Perot in 1988, four years after GM bought EDS. He had become frustrated at the slow pace of change at GM and how the leaders were being ineffective at leading the company through the difficult issues GM was facing. His quote is "If you see a snake, just kill it - don't appoint a committee on snakes." Some could say that is a short term view – just kill the snake you see now. But what about the flaw that is allowing the snakes to get in? The wise leader deals with both issues, but in the right order. Kill the snake, put out the fire, stop the bleeding, whatever cliché you want to use, and then deal with prevention of future snakes.

Therefore, one of your values needs to be driving the team and organization to get better - i.e. continuous improvement. So, after the snake is dead, then turn your attention to the nest of snakes and figure out how it got there in the first place. Then take actions to keep that kind of snake away, because a new breed of snake (problem) is just around the corner. One of the tenet's of Murphy's Law is that, "Nature always sides with the hidden flaw". The hidden flaws will enable more snakes to always come in. So, how you deal with the new snakes in a positive, focused, prioritized, and action-oriented manner (or not) is a reflection of your values. Your values (good or bad) will be reflected in the actions of your organization.

However, it is important for a leaders to <u>not</u> get the reputation (i.e. your brand, see chapter 8) as <u>only</u> being a "snake killer" – meaning you are usually dealing with the negative, which will impact your persona to the team. Your "snake killer" brand means you are usually the bearer of bad news. So, to your people, it may be a good day for them, when you do <u>not</u> come around. When people dread seeing you walking down the hallway and hope you do NOT stop to talk to them, it is a sign that you may be focusing too much on the negative. Do not get addicted to killing snakes or fighting fires. Because if that is where you get your "high", then you will look for snakes to kill and fires to fight in any minor issue that arises in the business. It is important that, even through all the fire-fighting and snake disposal work, you sustain and reinforce a reputation as a positive and optimistic leader. Maintain a balanced perspective. So, if it comes to pass that, to you, it seems the snakes are winning and the fires are getting hotter, and that is making you a negative, pessimistic leader. Then do everyone a favor, including yourself, and move on.

The final thought on this wisdom: you are in a leadership role to actually get something done – like handling the tough issues. Dealing with bad news and problems is part of your job to get resolved. The wise leader addresses problems head-on to get them out of way, so the team can focus on moving the organization forward. Keep in mind your role, primarily, is to make the organization better. You are there to help the organization thrive and become great in an unforgiving world. Not simply to be the caretaker for the status quo. Life is short, and your opportunity to lead and have an impact is even shorter. Be a leader who makes it happen, not just waits for it to happen. Also, celebrate and communicate when you and the team do make good things happen, even the little things. Appreciate and treasure those rare days that contain no drama. Appreciate the team who helped make the day boring by just doing their jobs really well. Then you will have people who come in each day to do great work for the team and the company and make good things happen with you.

REFLECTION:

Review the conversations of the day. Are they all on bad news or problems? Have you communicated anything positive or said "thanks"?

What did you get done this week? What did you cross off your to do list?

What snake did you kill this week? Whom on your team killed a snake – and did you say "thanks"?

What snakes are still alive and well in your organization, and living quite comfortably on your "to do" list? And you are continuing to ignore.

10

WISDOM #10

IF YOUR PEOPLE ARE NOT DOING WHAT YOU WANT, IT'S YOUR FAULT

Remember Wisdom #2 – Leaders are in charge. Your manager is expecting you to "own your results". You might as well accept this wisdom head-on. So, we close this conversation with repeating the principles of accountability, courage, and ownership for the results of the organization.

When people fall short, do not first ask - where did THEY go wrong? Ask FIRST, what <u>did I not</u> do to set this person or team up for success? Remember that while your people bring the needed set of skills and knowledge to the job, (if they do not, then why did you hire them?), it is the environment you create and perpetuate that engages them in a way to bring forth their best and help the team succeed. James Autry stated that leaders create a place where people can do great work. So, your job is to build the environment, give them the tools, direction, support, love, and feedback to enable their success. Next, be really smart, and get out of their way of their drive and talent. But, let them know when they hit target or by how much they missed with honest feedback, delivered with respect and caring.

Also, a bit of a side note here. Did you notice I used the word "love" a few sentences ago? There are probably some folks reading this that squirmed just a bit at the thought of bringing the concept of love into the workplace and relating it to the role of the leader. You will likely increase the odds of getting the results you need from your team if they truly know you care about them and their success – as people, not just names on an org chart. Maybe there is a variation on the concept of love that defines the honor, respect, trust, caring, and emotional connection that wise leaders work to build and maintain with each individual on their teams. Take the time to determine how you want to connect with your people and at more than just a manager/subordinate level. Keep in mind, that a deeper level of connection of people can be uncomfortable because it can make the tough conversations even tougher. However, the wise leader develops the ability to be comfortable with being uncomfortable. It certainly is easier being a true cold autocratic "Mr. Spock" style of leader. However, that style, I think only brings part of the leader's humanity to the organization. Be a complete person with your team. Use both sides of the brain, and all of your heart. Make it natural for your team to want to get the results you need by connecting with them at a personal level. Yes, love your team.

Okay, back to what this chapter is about – getting results. Remember, people want to win, succeed, and accomplish things that will make themselves proud. If a person does not want to win, succeed, and accomplish something, then find out why, provide feedback and guidance, but then make the decision to rectify in some manner. It could be a hiring mistake, or there could be training issues, or a lack of communicating expectations, needed results and consequences. Give good feedback often. Turn the person around, or turn them out.

Accepting performance that is not up to the expectations of you and the team clearly communicates what you are willing to accept and your true values on people providing good work. But the wise leader hates to fire good people because the person's skills and abilities are not a match for the job, and does not take any real satisfaction from ridding the organization of people whose values or demeanor was toxic to the organization. However, that is part of the role of being an accountable leader.

So, help people win by communicating what winning looks like and also what all the factors are that comprise success for each person and team. Define the outcomes needed from the team that determines success. Ensure that each person knows what a great day, week, month, and year looks like for them and the team. What are the behaviors that you want people to exhibit for themselves and the team to provide value? Don't make people guess at what you want them to do because, odds are, they will guess wrong, because of their own mental models.

The behaviors, (and therefore VALUES) you may want to give clear guidance on what you expect might include:

o **Attitude** – Talk to people about how you expect them to interact with you, their team members, customers, etc. This is the expectation to be a positive influence in the organization.

o **Accountability for results** – After all, each person was hired to actually do something. Communicate their ownership for the results they produce.

o **Dealing with adversity** – Because there will be tough times that will test your character and values. Define how you want them to react.

o **Dealing with each other** – And handling the human shortcoming and frailties we ALL have with patience, respect, and understanding.

o **Knowing the business** – People should have an expectation to know what the organization, at the micro and macro levels defines as success. Know who the customer is for the overall business and then for the value delivered by their specific team.

o **Truly be a part of the team**. – Even though their career desires may take them beyond their current role, have passion and commitment to doing a great job in their current role and helping others also be successful.

Define your expectations, communicate them early and often, and reinforce them in team meetings, one-on-ones, performance reviews, and with positive recognition. Connect the dots between the expectations and the results of the team.

What follows is a set of expectations I have communicated to my team in the leadership roles I have had over the years.

MY EXPECTATIONS

This is intended to answer the question, "What does Gary expect us to do?" Some of what you read may be high level and/or somewhat abstract in detail, but I think you should understand my thinking. I do want to get a list from you all as well that would tell me, "What does the team expect of me?" To me, these are good guidelines to make you into a valuable employee and help us grow into a successful and enjoyable team. In no particular order:

o **Speed** – Have a sense of urgency about your work. This company is always looking for ways to elevate our level of service to our external customers to make the company a preferred provider of our services. Therefore, the IT professionals – whether an employee or a contractor, in this company need to find that higher gear personally to deliver great service faster.

o **Patience & Tolerance** – The opposite at times of the above bullet. Rome was not built in a day, and neither will the long-term success of this department. People, (especially me), will make mistakes and dumb decisions at time. We are a business that has financial constraints, so we will never have an unlimited budget. That is just a reality.

o **Flexibility** – Be willing to wear many hats. We may need you to help out on projects or support in ways that may be beyond just writing or designing software.

o **Continual Learning** – If you are not reading about, exploring or playing with new technologies, you are not doing yourself or the department any favors, (especially yourself). People with successful careers in just about any endeavor have a strong curiosity about the "technology" of their job. Invest in yourself. Give me ideas on how to invest in you.

o **Passion for your Career** – This point ties to the bullet above. Hopefully you still get a buzz from your chosen field.

o **No Blinders** – Work and have influence beyond your own assignments. A "personal success, but a team failure" is highly unlikely to ever happen. Your success is tied to team and department success. The group you are in and the areas you are supporting should be wildly successful.

o **Know your Customer** – No matter what you are doing, somebody is using the output of your efforts for something of value. Know who that someone is, and understand their point of view. Credibility can be built on the successful delivery of defined services – we know exactly what we do for this problem and exactly what we deliver. "Customers", are teammates, project managers, internal clients, etc. The question you need to be able to answer to, "Who do I need to thrill today with the work I produce?"

o **Act like an Owner or Partner** – Look for opportunity for the department. Think like your personal financial success depends on the success of this department – which, by the way, might be true.

o **Be able to Present Yourself** – I need to be able to rely on anyone of you to meet with a customer, and maybe even make a short presentation or demo. Now, I will never knowingly put you in a position to fail with the above task with a presentation to a user that you may not be comfortable doing. However, this also means being able & willing to present yourself to me – so if you have questions, concerns, complaints, ideas - come talk to me. Don't just stew about it – just come talk to me. However, have the maturity to realize I may not give you an answer you will like.

o **Be a Positive Influence** – Having fun is always more helpful to everyone than whining. Spreading negativity provides <u>no value</u> to the team or our users. Stress burns out people and organizations. You have a right to think as negatively as you want. But you don't get to be "carrier" of pessimism to your teammates and bring anyone else down into your own morass. Ever. Pessimism and attitude need to stop at the tip of your nose.

o **Have the Desire and Enthusiasm to Build Something Great** – If you are satisfied with the way things are, then it may be time to move on. If you are relying on me to provide all the creativity, ideas, solutions, etc., we're in a bit of trouble. I need the brain power, energy, and investment of everyone to be thinking for and with me on how to grow this department. Ideas, suggestions, "what ifs", critical thinking, controlled discontent, are all the catalysts behind the growth of a team and a business. You are all closer to the technical realities of your jobs than I am so you have a valuable and relevant perspective.

The wise leader thinks holistically about what the team and organization needs people to do well day in and day out and then tailors those needs into clear and communicated expectations for people to guide them each day.

The final thought on this wisdom: your people really do want know what it takes to be successful. Be clear and be positive with your expectations. Your expectations should be focused on what to do, rather than what NOT to do. Defining your expectation as "negatives" (what not to do) communicates what will essentially get you punished for not following. That approach will not create and sustain a positive and engaging culture over the long term. So, be positive and communicate the guidelines of success, so your people love working for you, and then also love working for the organization, and come in each day to do great work for the team and the company. There's that "love" word again.

REFLECTIONS:

Did you get done what you expected to get done this week?

So, what do you expect your people to do and/or not do? Are your expectations a mystery to them? Have you ever asked if they knew your expectations?

Do they know, really know, what doing a good job really looks like in your eyes?

11

WRAP IT UP

WE HOLD THESE WISDOMS
TO BE SELF-EVIDENT

Yes, I am shamelessly stealing from one of the greatest documents ever written. Not that I am even hinting that what you have just read is even in the same literary universe as the United States Declaration of Independence. Because it is not, by light-years. However, I want to point out that the words, concepts, values, and beliefs from that Declaration of Independence, written over 200 years ago, are still relevant today, more than ten generations removed from its creation. My hope is that I have made the case that a set of leadership values and philosophies created less than 50 years ago, can still be valuable guidance to leaders of the 21st century.

Even though the "torch" of leadership in businesses and organizations, large and small, is being passed from my generation to those that follow, how to treat people and the blocking and tackling of effective and positive leadership has not fundamentally changed. The values and leadership behaviors presented here may be "old school" because they were born in a generation that has passed the baton.

However, these values and behaviors are still relevant because the nature of today's workforce has not fundamentally changed in terms of their <u>humanity</u>. Yes, today's workforce values different styles of communication and have a different definition of what success and happiness means to them, and they may have different priorities, but people are still people. People still want to be treated with respect, valued for who they are and for the talents that make them special and unique, and then given opportunities to succeed and **have meaning in their lives**. That last phrase is critically important for a leader to internalize – people in the generations following the boomers also want their lives to have mattered. People treasure being led by effective, honest, and values-based, visionary leaders whose focus is on having the organization and team <u>do great things</u>. These wise leaders will help their people succeed and have careers that mattered. Regardless of the generation, the leadership skills, behaviors, and values based on the leadership wisdoms explained here will <u>serve</u> your people well and build great teams.

Organizations still need people to "deliver the goods," especially when they are in formal leadership roles. Leaders still get work done through the brain power, dedication, work, and passion of people – day in and day out. It is not all that complicated. However, leaders have a tendency to make it complicated because they operate from a "me-focused" mentality, rather than an external focus on making their teams and managers highly effective in their roles. Focus on the team in order to have those teams deliver great value to the larger organization from the work they produce. Build great teams to enable organizations be highly effective and deliver great value to whomever is defined as their customers and stakeholders. Leaders need to do this just to enable organizations to <u>survive</u>.

But, an organization's goal is not just survival. The goal is to thrive in the marketplace in which they compete and build greatness to be passed on to the next generation of leaders.

Today's leaders, more than my generation, will deal with a greater magnitude and speed of the disruption of technology and social change. But, you probably already knew that. So, a new hat for today's leader's to wear is that of organizational change manager. These leadership wisdoms build a trustworthiness and credibility that is essential for successfully leading a team through change. People need to know they are being dealt with honesty and truth to reduce their perception of the risk to them personally from the change. The team needs to know their leader will be there right beside them to walk through the mine field of change.

Most organizational change takes place in a social context and evokes emotions associated with the perceived loss of a safe environment – in front of other people, who, by human nature, will be judging them. So, everyone's boat is being rocked. The wise leader knows they need their stars to help bring the entire team through. They also know the organization is looking to them to produce the results needed from the team to support the change. But, the "current" ways are easy and comfortable, and the "new" ways are hard and often uncomfortable. People will fail more and make more mistakes with the new ways and they prefer not to fail, so they will exhibit rational behavior and resist the change. People get a sense of accomplishment and pride from doing what they have always done well for quite some time. They are smart enough to know they will most likely lose more personally than they will gain from whatever is changing. So, sensing there is no personal benefit and only personal loss, people naturally resist change.

Wise leaders understand all the dynamics that align against successfully implementing change. Wise leaders also realize no wonderful document, no passionate speech, no all-hands town hall, or consultant explaining the change can really counteract all the negative "physics" lining up against an organizational change effort. Change is often threatening. Only trustworthy, involved, and supportive leadership will overcome the organizational inertia poised to stomp all over the big and little evolutionary and, maybe even revolutionary, changes needed for the organization to <u>thrive</u>.

So, wise and effective leadership helps facilitate change and organizational success because:

o   The leader starts with honesty and openness (#1).

o   Adds in truly being accountable for results (#2).

o   Is accountable to stop low/negative value actions (#3).

o   Understands that they and the world are both imperfect. So tough but perhaps imperfect decisions are often needed (#4).

o   Knows that organizations are dependent on good people to do great work to succeed (#5).

o   Realizes they will never have all the right answers and need to include the thinking of the best people (#6).

o   Operates from a mindset of focus and ownership for the results their team needs to produce (#7).

o   Accepts that people are looking for them to define and then demonstrate the values for the organization (#8).

o   Grasps that they are in their role to get results. Not just think great things, but to deliver great things (#9).

o   Thinks holistically and connects the results from their people to the expectations they define and values they communicate every day (#10).

Wisdom is acquired through practice, constant attention, strong self-awareness, and the acceptance that you will never be perfect. Like the people you are leading, you are flawed. So, even the wisest of leaders will have a lot of off days. You will not get everything (or maybe anything) right each and every day. Mistakes, by you, are just part of a leadership role. You will get angry over trivial stuff. You will forget to say "thanks" because you are accustomed to your people doing good work. You will get caught up in the manic life within the organization and let the situation control you and tarnish the values you want to express through your actions. You will make mistakes, probably every day. That's life. Learn from yourself. Forgive yourself, and move on.

I encourage you to understand that leadership is not a job, but rather a vocation and stewardship because you are impacting people's lives. It is a calling. Continue to learn the craft. Read the thinking on leadership of men and women who are really the powerful and wise thinkers of our day on this topic. Learn from Marshall Goldsmith, Stephen Covey, Barry Posner, James Kouzes, Warren Bennis, Frances Hesselbein, James Autry, Robert Greenleaf, Ken Blanchard, Meg Wheatley, John Maxwell, and many more. Expand your thinking and understanding of leadership to expand your own leadership capacity. So you can increase the leadership capacity in your organization, one engaged and passionate employee at a time.

So, **please** do not let this be the last book on leadership you ever read. Honestly and candidly - that would be really dumb.

I would close with "Good luck," but wise and effective leaders create their own luck. Their luck is created through consistent high performing leadership skills that create passionate, engaged, and empowered teams who love their work, their peers, their leaders, and the organization.

Wise leaders evolve to view their role as a stewardship to serve their team to engage the minds, talents, and, yes, truly the hearts of the people who view you as their leader. That style of leadership is truly a beautiful thing to behold.

So, then you will have talented, enthused, and engaged people who come in each day to do great work for the team and the company.

FINAL REFLECTION:

So, what will you do differently tomorrow? How will you begin to review your own performance each day and give yourself feedback?

What is the one behavior or action you will change to use Old School Wisdoms in your work place and with your team?

GRASS ROOTS WISDOMS

1. Be honest, upfront, and candid

2. Leaders are in charge

3. Leaders are not obligated to perpetuate foolishness. And expected to stop it. See #2.

4. Leaders must choose which problem(s) to live with. There are very few perfect solutions.

5. Run the company (i.e. your team or organization) so the best people love it.

6. Sit in the grandstand. Get all the perspectives on the situation.

7. Run your business/team/project like it's your company. Is it important enough that you would pay for it?

8. No second chance to make a first impression. However, you are always making an impression.

9. Bad news, unlike wine and cheese, does not get better with age. Corollary: See snake → kill snake. See #'s 1, 2, and 3 above.

10. If your people are not doing what you want, it's your fault. See #2 above.

BIBLIOGRAPHY

Autry, James. For Love and Profit: The Art of Caring Leadership. New York: Morrow, 1990. Print.

Collins, James C., and Jerry I. Porras. Built to Last: Successful Habits of Visionary Companies. Paperback, Harper Business Essentials, 2004. Print.

Green, David W. "Confirmation Bias, Problem-Solving and Cognitive Models." Advances in Psychology (1990): 553-62.

Greenleaf, Robert K. Servant Leadership: A Journey into the Nature of Legitimate Power and Greatness. New York: Paulist, 1977. Print.

Perot, Henry Ross, and Thomas Moore. "The GM System is Like a Blanket of Fog" Fortune 15 Feb. 1988: n. pag. Print.

Rehak, Judith. "Tylenol Made a Hero of Johnson & Johnson: The Recall That Started." International Herald Tribune. The New York Times, 23 Mar. 2002. Web.

Senge, Peter M. The Fifth Discipline: The Art and Practice of the Learning Organization. New York: Doubleday/Currency, 1990. Print.

Taiichi Ohno; Toyota Production System: Beyond Large-Scale Production. Portland, OR: Productivity Press, 1988. Print

ABOUT THE AUTHOR

Gary Hassenstab has been in a variety of leadership roles within technology organizations for over 30 years. He has led organizations ranging from 10 to 100 technical professionals in the banking, global IT services, engineering, pharmaceutical automation, and freight logistics industries.

In order to learn more about leadership and effective management, Gary took a timeout from formal leadership roles and spent 5 years in leadership development as a facilitator of leadership and management courses. In addition, Gary's role was also to analyze the results of a values and competency-based assessment tool and conduct coaching sessions with the participants. He conducted over 400 individual assessment and coaching sessions and numerous coaching sessions with intact leadership teams. Gary was also selected to be a leadership analyst and coach for the EDS Executive Development program. His role was identify the experience and skill gaps for the participants and prepare targeted coaching and feedback to accelerate their readiness to take on senior leadership roles.

51276011R00048

Made in the USA
Lexington, KY
01 September 2019